Katelyn Ohashi

The Gymnastics Star for kids

Daisy Katy

Copyright

Table of Contents

Introduction

Not only for her amazing gymnastics ability, but also for the happiness, enthusiasm, and positivity she infuses into everything she does, Katelyn Ohashi makes people all around grin. Born in Seattle, Washington, on April 12, 1997, Katelyn was a bright and energetic girl who loved to jump, dance, and flip about her house from the moment she could walk. Early on, Katelyn was gifted in gymnastics; by the time she was a small child, she was already fantasizing about swooping into the air like her gymnastics heroes.

Katelyn started her trip into the realm of gymnastics at just three years old. Her parents decided to register her in gymnastics lessons after noticing her great vitality to enable her to focus that energy in a constructive way. Little did they know that this would set off something rather remarkable. Katelyn fell fast in love with the sport and practiced her skills, honed her beam balance, and perfected her flips and twists for hours. She was natural, and her coaches quickly came to see she might be among the greatest.

Katelyn's commitment to gymnastics strengthened as she got older. She trained for hours every day and put forth much effort, and her talent drove her to the top ranks of her sport. Katelyn was traveling to contests, winning gold, and challenging some of the top gymnasts in the world by the time she was a teen. At the age of 15, she even won the esteemed American Cup, a significant achievement that set her in a position to maybe qualify for the Olympics.

But Katelyn's road wasn't without difficulties. She started to suffer from the pressure to be perfect in her appearance as much as in her routines. She pushed herself till it finally caused her body to malfunction. She had major injuries, including torn shoulders and a damaged back, which caused her to pause the sport she loved. Along with the emotional strain she experienced, these injuries caused Katelyn to wonder if she wanted to keep doing gymnastics overall.

Katelyn never lost her love of the sport in these hard times. She decided to quit the demanding world of competitive gymnastics and enroll in UCLA, where she joined the gymnastics team after spending time resting and rehabilitating. Katelyn discovered happiness at UCLA—something she hadn't felt in a long time. Freed from the demands of elite-level competition, she regained her passion for gymnastics and started to concentrate on expressing herself and having fun with her routines.

Katelyn developed the floor routine that would transform her life while still a student at UC. She stunned the globe in 2018 with a routine that included flips, twists, and even some dancing to a medley of Michael Jackson songs. Her daily schedule was so vibrant and joyful that it soon went viral and attracted millions of views online along with compliments from all around the globe. The judges equally delighted Katelyn with a flawless score of 10.0! The way Katelyn's performance made everyone who watched it smile, however, made this event especially memorable—not only in terms of score.

Katelyn's narrative spans more ground than only gymnastics. It's about conquering obstacles, rediscovering yourself, and spreading your enthusiasm to others. Katelyn never gave up on what she loved even after suffering major injuries and sport-related pressures. Rather, she discovered a means to make gymnastics her own, transforming it into something that would bring her—and millions of others—pure delight.

Katelyn Ohashi is today not just for her amazing gymnastics ability but also for her good attitude and dedication to disseminating ideas of self-love, body acceptance, and mental health consciousness. For young athletes and anyone who has ever overcome obstacles in their lives, she is now a role model. Katelyn's narrative reminds us all that actual success is about being happy, loyal to yourself, and doing what you love with all your heart—not only about medals.

Chapter 1:Childhood in Seattle: A Little Girl with Big Dreams

Born on April 12, 1997, Katelyn Ohashi's tale starts in the wet metropolis of Seattle, Washington. Katelyn was vibrantly alive even as a small child. She delighted in bouncing about the living room, jumping off furniture, and whirling—sometimes to the point that her parents questioned whether she would ever stop! Katelyn was a natural-born gymnast, her limitless energy and love of flipping and spinning around obvious proof. She was not just any child.

Early on, Katelyn's parents saw her aptitude; they registered her for gymnastics classes when she was barely three years old. Katelyn fell in love with the sport not very slowly. On the mats, beams, and bars, she felt right at home; she was always eager to pick up fresh motions. Katelyn was little, but her coaches saw she had a unique spark—she was fearless, driven, and ready to try even the most difficult flips and stunts.

Katelyn's love of gymnastics grew only as she kept practicing and developing. She worked in the gym for hours honing her routines and fantasizing about becoming the reigning champion. Katelyn, unlike many children her age, enjoyed the hard effort rather than finding it objectionable. She delighted in nailing a challenging routine, the excitement of learning something new, and the freedom to express herself through movement. For Katelyn, gymnastics was more than simply a sport; it was a means of channeling her aspirations and vitality into something spectacular.

Katelyn, who grew up in Seattle, had great aspirations of one day taking the front stage internationally. Looking up at the gymnastics stars on TV, she visualized herself turning and flipping before thousands of applauding spectators. Her imagination was as strong as her aptitude, and she never ceased believing she could reach whatever her intellect could grasp.

Katelyn, however, was still a young child who loved to have fun even if she had great aspirations. She delighted in hanging out with her family, playing with friends, and discovering the lovely parks and outdoor areas all around Seattle. Her early years were full of the kind of excursions only a small girl with a great imagination could dream about.

Katelyn's gymnastics passion grew as she aged, along with her skills. She started to stand out in contests, and it became evident that her grand aspirations might very well come true. Katelyn was one step closer to becoming the gymnastics star she had always dreamed of with every turn, every leap, every grin.

Katelyn Ohashi's early years in Seattle were the start of an amazing trip full of diligence, willfulness, and the conviction that, given the heart to pursue a dream, none is too large.

Chapter 2:Joining the Elite Gymnastics World

Growing older, Katelyn Ohashi's gymnastics ability became impossible to overlook. Katelyn had been causing waves in the gymnastics scene by the time she was barely twelve years old. Her routines were more courageous, her flips higher, and her commitment unparalleled. She was growing to be among the most gifted young gymnasts in the nation, not simply a tiny Seattle child.

Everything grew more rigorous when Katelyn entered the elite gymnastics scene. Like the major leagues of the sport, elite gymnastics features just the absolute best athletes. It meant working harder, facing the best gymnasts in the nation, and executing routines more challenging than ever before. Still, Katelyn was ready for the difficulty. She practiced every flip, twist, and landing until they were just right spending hours every day in the gym.

For someone so young, Katelyn was already participating on the U.S. national team at 15, a great feat. Representing her nation and challenging the top gymnasts from around the globe, she made trips to events all around. One of the most elite gymnastics events worldwide, the American Cup in 2013 paid dividends for Katelyn's diligence. Her dream of maybe competing in the Olympics was one she had harbored since she was a small child, and her triumph set her on that road.

But the world of competitive gymnastics was not focused just on medals and glory. It was also a site of great pressure. The routines were demanding, and the judges observed every action searching for the smallest errors. Additionally under a lot of strain was to always be perfect and to look in a specific manner. For Katelyn, the weight seemed occasionally unbearable. She aimed to be the best, but the relentless pursuit of excellence began to wear her down on the inside as much as the outward.

Katelyn started to struggle as she pushed herself even harder. She suffered major injuries including torn shoulders and a cracked back. Her pain made it challenging for her to keep up with the rigorous training regimen; thus, she had to make the difficult choice to stop gymnastics. For Katelyn, who had put so much effort toward the top, it was a terrible period. She realized, though, that before she could resume the sport she loved, she had to tend to her body and her mind.

Notwithstanding the difficulties, Katelyn's time in competitive gymnastics gave her invaluable insights into endurance, fortitude, and the need to listen to her body. She discovered that although winning was thrilling, she still needed to look for herself and find delight in her work. As she entered the next phase of her gymnastics adventure, these teachings would grow even more crucial.

Although Katelyn Ohashi had highs and lows in the top gymnastics scene, she also underwent amazing development. She discovered what it means to be committed to her trade and how to juggle her aspirations with her health throughout these years. Though the road was difficult, Katelyn's experience in competitive gymnastics was crucial in determining the athlete and person she would grow to be.

Transition to UCLA

Katelyn Ohashi found herself at a crossroads following major injuries and the extreme demands of elite gymnastics. She had spent so much of her life doing gymnastics, but the physical and psychological toll had left her questioning whether she could keep on in the sport. She needed breaks for her health, but they also allowed her time to consider what made her happy.

Katelyn decided during this period that would alter everything: she decided to join the gymnastics team of one of the best colleges in the nation, UCLA. Along with its academics, UCLA boasts one of the greatest college gymnastics teams in the country, run under the direction of the venerable coach Valorie Kondos Field, sometimes referred to as "Miss Val." This choice was about finding a new road that let Katelyn rekindle her passion for gymnastics on her terms, not only about keeping on her present course.

Katelyn was welcomed into a team at UCLA stressing happiness, originality, and creativity. The emphasis was on appreciating the process and praising each gymnast's particular talents rather than only on winning. To Katelyn, this was a breath of fresh air. She was now part of a team that respected her for who she was, not only how flawless her routines could be after years of experiencing the great pressure of elite competition.

Katelyn's confidence was rebuilt and her love of gymnastics was rediscovered through training at UCLA. She stopped having to worry about satisfying others' standards or about being flawless. She was urged instead to be herself, to have fun, and to let her performance reflect her personality. These fresh surroundings rekindled Katelyn's love of the sport and helped her rehabilitate physically and emotionally.

Coach Val helped Katelyn flourish. She started doing technically flawless but also highly energetic and creatively inspired routines. Gymnastics became Katelyn's means of self-expression, a means of connecting with audiences and sharing her passion for the sport. She was having fun once more, and her performance of every routine revealed this.

Katelyn's choice to pick UCLA and welcome this new phase of her gymnastics career paid off handsomely in 2018. Millions of people all around the globe were moved by her viral floor routine. The program honored what Katelyn had rediscovered at UCLA—joy, freedom, and the pure love of gymnastics. More importantly, her performance reminded everyone that gymnastics is about the enthusiasm and delight the sport can provide, not only about points.

Katelyn's decision to enroll in UCLA and join their gymnastics team was motivated by more than just carrying on her athletic career. It was about discovering her, rediscovering what delighted her, and writing a fresh chapter full of self-expression and optimism. Katelyn not only became a champion but also discovered the freedom to be herself at UCLA, demonstrating that occasionally the finest decisions are those that let us rediscover the things we most enjoy.

Chapter 3 The Viral Floor Routine

The viral floor routine of Katelyn Ohashi is the stuff of legend—a moment in gymnastics history that will live in millions of hearts all around. The sheer delight and excitement Katelyn brought to the floor, reminding everyone why we initially fell in love with athletics, made it so unique, not just the amazing flips, turns, and dance skills.

The background of the viral routine begins at UCLA when Katelyn was rediscovering her passion for gymnastics. She was having fun once more free from the demands of elite competition; that fun was going to be shared with the whole planet. January 2019 found

Katelyn performing at a collegiate meet in Anaheim, California. Something wonderful happened the instant she set foot on the floor.

The music started—a vibrant blend of Michael Jackson hits—and Katelyn filled the arena with her contagious grin. This was a unique routine from the first move. Katelyn danced, she grooved, and she carried the audience along on the ride rather than merely following her schedule. Though every flip and turn was accomplished flawlessly, what distinguished it was the attitude, the enthusiasm, and the pure delight. Katelyn's routine celebrated gymnastics and herself.

The throng went crazy as Katelyn danced her way across the floor. As she precisely and stylishly nailed every detail, the judges marveled. The whole crowd burst in cheers and ovation when she came to her last position. Without delay, the judges gave her a flawless 10.0—a mark every gymnast dreams of. Still, the event transcended mere score to include more. It was about Katelyn's demeanor toward everyone else observing. She had transformed a gymnastics program into an energetic, engaging, and emotionally charged show.

The program transcended the confines of that stadium. Social media helped Katelyn's performance rapidly go viral and travel like wildfire over the internet. Millions of people all around had watched it within days, and everyone was talking about the gymnast who reminded the globe what delight in athletics looks like. Fans, sportsmen, and celebrities all shared the routine, and Katelyn shot to overnight popularity.

Still, Katelyn's performance made a potent statement beyond the viral glory. It demonstrated that gymnastics and sports in general are not only about excellence or medal counting. They are about expressing yourself, having fun, and faithfully doing what you love. That schedule, for Katelyn, represented her path from the demands of professional gymnastics to discovering her bliss at UCLA. It was an honoring of who she had grown to be and a reminder that the most significant triumphs are the ones that let you feel alive.

Katelyn Ohashi's viral floor routine is more than simply a gymnastics highlight; it's a moment that delighted millions of people worldwide. It reminded everyone that the best performances are those from the heart and demonstrated that actual success results from being genuine to yourself.

The Gymnastics Style of Katelyn

Combining amazing athleticism with expressive dancing and a joyous attitude that distinguishes Katelyn Ohashi from other gymnasts, her gymnastics approach is as unique and vivid as she is. Katelyn was well-known from early on for her strong, dynamic routines that fused challenging skills with a sense of artistry and personality to create outstanding performances.

Katelyn's gymnastics technique is among the most remarkable in that she can effortlessly mix grace with force. Her powerful tumbling passes, high-flying flips, and twists that astound the viewers are well-known. Her routines are very unique, though, because she combines dancing techniques and expressions that highlight her joyful and creative side with these demanding components. Katelyn's motions are always crisp, exact, and alive whether she is spinning on the floor or jumping through the air.

Particularly her floor routines became more to define her. She told a tale with every performance, not only going out there to exhibit her abilities. Her choreography was always vibrant, featuring winks, amusing dancing steps, and times when the audience might participate in the fun. Her performances were unforgettable because of her capacity to interact with the audience and include them in her performance. Seeing Katelyn on the floor seemed more like celebrating gymnastics than observing a sport.

Still, Katelyn's approach went beyond just audience entertainment. It also had to be about sharing her enthusiasm for the sport. Following the demands of professional gymnastics, Katelyn discovered a fresh sense of freedom at UCLA, where she was urged to execute routines that honored her values and who she was. Her love of gymnastics rediscovered was made possible by this freedom, which also permeated every routine she executed. Reminding everyone that gymnastics could be as fun as it was demanding, her approach was bold, confident, and unquestioningly joyous.

Apart from her floor routines, Katelyn introduced her style to other competitions including the uneven bars and the balance beam. She kept her trademark smile while combining graceful postures and smooth transitions with bold flips and turns on the beam. She moved fluidly and powerfully on the bars, giving difficult skills seeming simplicity. Her routines, which highlighted her flexibility as a gymnast, always combined artistry and agility over all the events.

Katelyn's gymnastics approach reflects her personality—one of vitality, inventiveness, and a passion for life. She competed to share her excitement and passion with the world, not only to win. Her routines served as a reminder that gymnastics is an art of performance and self-expression as much as a technical ability test. Like Katelyn, many young gymnasts have been motivated to embrace their uniqueness and find delight in their performances by her approach.

Chapter 4:Life Beyond the Mat

For Katelyn Ohashi, life beyond the gym has been equally motivating as her gymnastics career. Katelyn left professional gymnastics and entered a new phase of her life where she keeps having a positive influence by using her platform to support significant causes and tell her story to the world.

Promoting body positivity and mental health awareness is one of the most important features of Katelyn's life outside of gymnastics. Over her gymnastics career, particularly during her tenure as an elite gymnast, Katelyn was under constant criticism for her beauty and the pressure to live up to impossible standards. These encounters drove her to battle mental health problems and body image concerns. Katelyn came out of these difficulties, nevertheless, with a fresh feeling of self-worth and a wish to support others who might be going through comparable difficulties.

Katelyn has started to actively promote body positivity, urging people to value their bodies and enjoy their particular features. Using her tale to inspire others to love themselves exactly as they are, she candidly discusses her own experiences with body shaming and the negative consequences of society's expectations. Using interviews, social media, and public speaking events, Katelyn emphasizes in her message—that true beauty results from confidence, self-love, and authenticity.

Apart from body acceptance, Katelyn is driven by mental health campaigning. She is personally aware of the negative effects on mental health that society's expectations and competition pressures can cause on a person. Through sharing her path, Katelyn hopes to reduce the stigma around mental health concerns and inspire others to get support and treatment when they most need it. She underlines the need for resilience, self-care, and appreciating the really important things.

Katelyn's impact reaches even her participation in several charitable endeavors. Working to help people live better, she supports groups emphasizing mental health, body image, and young empowerment. Katelyn is committed to change whether she's helping charities, coaching young athletes, or working with companies she shares ideals.

Katelyn has also embraced her roles as a writer and inspirational speaker. She travels the nation telling her tale to audiences of all ages, motivating them to keep true to themselves, follow their interests, and conquer obstacles. She engages with people on a deep and personal level and her presentations exude the same vitality and optimism that defined her gymnastics routines. To extend her message of empowerment and self-acceptance, Katelyn has also penned essays and pieces providing insights into her experiences.

Although gymnastics will always remain a part of Katelyn's life, she has discovered satisfaction in investigating other artistic directions. Poetry and writing are her passions; she frequently expresses her ideas and feelings in various media. Her poems capture her path of self-discovery and development, therefore providing a window into her inner world and the lessons she has discovered along the way.

Katelyn's life outside the mat is evidence of her tenacity, fortitude, and the need to keep true to herself. Using her voice to motivate good change in the world, she has converted her difficulties into chances to help others. For innumerable others, Katelyn is a source of inspiration whether she is promoting body positivity, mental health, or her narrative via public speaking and writing.

Her story reminds us that the various ways we develop, adjust, and discover fresh paths to happiness and fulfillment characterize our lives rather than one chapter. From a young gymnast striving for excellence to a strong, confident lady having a long-lasting influence much beyond the gymnastics floor,

Katelyn Ohashi's narrative is one of metamorphosis.

Returning to the Community

Katelyn Ohashi's dedication to returning to her community reflects her great awareness of the difficulties she has gone through and her will to assist others in conquering like difficulties. Rising to popularity with her viral gymnastics performance, Katelyn has utilized her position not only to tell her story but also to help other people live better. Whether she's supporting mental health projects, pushing body positivity, or motivating young athletes, Katelyn's attempts to give back are driven by a real enthusiasm for guiding others toward their routes to happiness and self-acceptance.

Among the most important ways Katelyn returns is by supporting body positivity. Having battled body image problems while a top gymnast, Katelyn is aware of the demands young people—especially young women—face about their looks. She has seized her experiences and transformed them into a potent declaration of self-love and acceptance. Katelyn candidly emphasizes the need to accept one's body and bucking unattainable beauty ideals. She tries to reach as many people as possible with public speaking, social media, and partnerships with companies emphasizing body image.

Katelyn also participates extensively in mental health advocacy. Understanding how mental health issues affect people, especially those in demanding fields like athletics, Katelyn has given supporting projects for mental well-being top importance. She regularly talks about her path with mental health, including her challenges as a gymnast and how she came to a better and happier place. Through candid sharing of her experiences, Katelyn encourages others to get the care they need and aims to reduce the stigma around mental health. She works with companies that emphasize mental health resources and education to make sure her message gets to people most in need.

Apart from her advocacy activities, Katelyn is driven to enable the following generation of sportsmen. She spends time working with young people through different events and initiatives since she knows the value of mentoring and direction in enabling young people to reach their dreams. Katelyn is dedicated to helping young athletes grow not only their physical abilities but also their confidence, resilience, and feeling of self-worth whether she is mentoring at gymnastics facilities, speaking at colleges, or supporting youth empowerment projects.

Beyond her activism, Katelyn's charitable endeavors go. She backs a range of humanitarian endeavors, including those with an eye toward social justice, equality, and schooling. She thinks of using her position to elevate the voices of underprivileged groups and to assist initiatives aiming at long-lasting constructive transformation. Often involved in awareness campaigns, charity auctions, and fundraising events, Katelyn uses her voice and power to support causes consistent with her ideals.

Katelyn stays rooted in the conviction that everyone has value and should be supported throughout all of her efforts. Her kindness, generosity, and sincere concern for others—qualities that show up in all spheres of her community involvement—are well-known. Katelyn's method of returning is based on actually and significantly improving the lives of those she interacts with, not on chasing praise or awards.

Katelyn Ohashi is a shining example of character and her will to use her accomplishments to inspire others seen by her devotion to returning to the community. Inspired many people to embrace their selves and to help one another on the road toward self-acceptance and mental well-being, she has converted her personal experiences into potent weapons for advocacy and change. Through her continuous work, Katelyn keeps having a positive influence and leaves a legacy of compassion, empowerment, and resiliency that will motivate the next generations.

Chapter 5:Fun Facts About Katelyn Ohashi

Here are some fun and lighthearted facts about Katelyn Ohashi:

1. A Gymnast at Three: Katelyn started gymnastics when she was just 3 years old! While most toddlers were figuring out how to walk without falling over, Katelyn was already flipping and tumbling like a pro.

2. Viral Queen: Katelyn's 2019 floor routine at UCLA went viral and racked up millions of views online. It's safe to say that more

people have watched her dance and flip than the latest blockbuster movie!

3. A Perfect 10—Over and Over: During her time at UCLA, Katelyn earned not just one, but multiple perfect 10s for her routines. She's the Beyoncé of gymnastics—flawless every time!

4. Music Moves Her: Katelyn's famous floor routine featured a medley of Michael Jackson hits, and she moonwalked her way right into gymnastics history. If gymnastics doesn't work out, she could always start a dance career!

5. Gymnastics isn't her only talent: Katelyn is also a talented writer and poet. She's known for writing beautiful and thoughtful pieces that explore everything from her gymnastics journey to her views on self-love and acceptance. Who knew she could tumble on the mat and with words?

6. She's a Foodie: Katelyn loves trying new foods, and she's not afraid to indulge her sweet tooth. Ice cream, cookies, and donuts are some of her favorites. After all, life's too short not to enjoy a treat now and then!

7. Go Team!: Katelyn has always been a team player. During her time at UCLA, she wasn't just focused on her success—she was also the

ultimate cheerleader for her teammates, always supporting them and lifting their spirits.

8. A Creative Soul: In addition to gymnastics and writing, Katelyn has a passion for art. She enjoys drawing and painting as a way to relax and express herself off the mat. She's an all-around creative powerhouse!

9. Little Gymnast, Big Heart: Despite her big accomplishments, Katelyn remains humble and always makes time to give back. She's involved in various charities and is passionate about supporting body positivity and mental health awareness.

10. Celebrity Shoutouts: When her routine went viral, Katelyn received praise from celebrities like Chrissy Teigen and Janet Jackson. Not many people can say they've impressed both an Olympic panel and Hollywood stars!

11. A Different Kind of Competition: Katelyn has faced off against some tough competitors in gymnastics, but did you know she also once went head-to-head with a pancake? That's right—she competed in a pancake-eating contest, proving she can handle challenges both on and off the mat!

12. Inspirational Speaker: Katelyn uses her voice to inspire others through motivational

speaking. She travels the country, sharing her journey and encouraging people to love themselves and chase their dreams. It turns out she's just as inspiring with a microphone as she is with a floor routine.

Katelyn Ohashi isn't just an incredible gymnast—she's a multi-talented, creative, and kind-hearted individual who knows how to have fun and inspire others wherever she goes!

Messages for Young Athletes

Here are some motivational and encouraging messages for young athletes, inspired by Katelyn Ohashi's journey:

1. "Believe in your magic." Katelyn's incredible journey reminds us that everyone has something special inside them. Trust in your abilities and let your unique talents shine, whether on the field, the court, or the mat.

2. "It's okay to stumble—as long as you keep getting back up." Katelyn faced injuries and setbacks, but she didn't let them stop her. Remember, it's not about how many times you fall, but how many times you get back up and keep pushing forward.

3. "Have fun and be yourself." Katelyn’s routines were so memorable because she had fun and let her personality shine. Don’t forget to enjoy what you do and show the world who you are. Your passion and joy are just as important as your skills.

4. "You are more than your scores." Gymnastics taught Katelyn that it’s not just about perfect scores—what matters most is how you feel about yourself. Remember that your worth isn’t defined by trophies or medals but by who you are inside.

5. *1"Support your teammates—your success is theirs too." Katelyn was known for

cheering on her teammates just as much as she focused on her performance. Celebrate your friends' victories and lift each other. Together, you're stronger.

6. "Listen to your body and mind." Katelyn learned the hard way how important it is to take care of herself. Pay attention to what your body and mind are telling you. Rest when you need to, and remember that taking care of yourself is part of being a champion.

7. Let your passion guide you."Katelyn's love for gymnastics is what helped her through tough times. Whatever sport you play, do it because you love it, and let that passion drive

you to keep improving and enjoying every moment.

8. "Embrace your imperfections." No one is perfect, and that's okay. Katelyn's journey shows us that it's our imperfections that make us unique and interesting. Don't be afraid to embrace who you are, flaws and all.

9. It's never too late to find your joy again." Even if you feel burnt out or discouraged, like Katelyn once did, know that you can always find your way back to what you love. Don't be afraid to take a break, explore new things, and rediscover what makes you happy.

10. "Remember to smile." Katelyn’s smile lit up every room and every routine. No matter what challenges you face, keep smiling and spreading positivity. Your smile can be just as powerful as any skill you master.

These messages, inspired by Katelyn Ohashi’s journey, remind young athletes that success isn’t just about winning—it's about joy, resilience, self-expression, and supporting others along the way.

Gymnastics Drills Inspired by Katelyn

Sure! Here's a fun and playful twist on gymnastics drills inspired by Katelyn Ohashi's joyful style:

1. Dance Like No One's Watching

Purpose: Get creative and show off your dance moves while building confidence.

How to Do It:

- Pick your favorite song—something that makes you want to dance!
- Create a mini-routine with at least two fun dance moves and a simple tumbling pass, like a cartwheel or roundoff.

- Add your flair—make funny faces, do a silly spin, or throw in a dab! The goal is to have fun and let your personality shine, just like Katelyn did in her viral routines.
- Invite a friend or teammate to join in and have a dance-off to see who can create the most entertaining routine!

2. Superhero Landings

Purpose: Practice sticking your landings like a superhero.

How to Do It:

- Imagine you're a superhero landing after flying through the sky! Practice doing big jumps, tuck jumps, or back handsprings, and land with a strong, dramatic pose—maybe one knee down, one fist to the floor, just like they do in the movies!

- Hold your superhero pose for 3 seconds while saying, “I’ve got this!”

- Challenge yourself to stick your landing every time. If you wobble, just get back up and try again—superheroes never give up!

3. Leap for the Stars

Purpose: Make your leaps feel as light and exciting as jumping on the moon.

How to Do It:

- Pretend the floor is made of trampoline springs. Take a running start and leap as high as you can, reaching for the stars.

- As you leap, imagine you're catching stars in your hands—grab as many as you can!

- End each leap with a twirl or a funny pose, like pretending to juggle all the stars you've caught.

- See who in your group can leap the highest or catch the most "stars" in one go!

4. Balance Beam Dance Party

Purpose: Practice balance while having a mini dance party on the beam.

How to Do It:

- Choose a favorite upbeat song and imagine the balance beam is your dance floor.

- Start with a basic move, like walking or skipping on the beam, and add a dance move every few steps. Maybe a moonwalk, a shimmy, or even a floss!

- Strike a fun pose at the end of the beam—try balancing on one foot or doing a big wave to your imaginary fans.

- Play "Follow the Leader" with friends—one person does a dance move on the beam, and everyone else tries to copy it without falling off!

5. Tumbling Treasure Hunt

Purpose: Make tumbling practice into a fun treasure hunt.

How to Do It:

- Scatter small "treasures" (like colorful beanbags or stuffed animals) around your tumbling mat.

- Perform a tumbling pass—like a forward roll, cartwheel, or handspring—to reach a treasure, then collect it and bring it back to your starting spot.

- Try to collect as many treasures as you can without losing your balance or missing a step.

- Add a challenge by doing a funny dance or spin each time you collect a treasure. Whoever collects the most treasures with the silliest moves wins!

6. Beam Balancing Bonanza

Purpose: Practice balance while imagining the beam is something wacky.

How to Do It:

- Pretend the beam is something fun—like a narrow bridge over a river filled with crocodiles, or a tightrope between two skyscrapers!

- Practice walking across it carefully, doing small jumps or turns, while imagining the crocodiles snapping below or the city lights flashing far below.

- Make it a game by balancing with one hand on your head, or while pretending to juggle, and see how long you can stay on the beam.

- End with a dramatic leap to safety, with a big landing pose that shows you've conquered the challenge!

7. Freestyle Floor Fun

Purpose: Combine tumbling with your wildest, most creative dance moves.

How to Do It:

- Pick a favorite song and create a wild, fun floor routine that includes at least one tumbling pass, like a somersault or cartwheel.
- Add in your silliest dance moves—like a robot dance, a disco spin, or even pretending to be a cat or dinosaur for a few steps!
- The goal is to have fun, be as goofy as you like, and just let loose—think of it as a

chance to make everyone watching laugh and cheer.

- Perform your routine for friends or family, and see if they can copy your moves!

These drills are all about having fun while practicing gymnastics, just like Katelyn Ohashi did. They encourage creativity, self-expression, and, most importantly, enjoying every moment of your time in the gym!

Q&A: Test Your Knowledge

Here's a fun Q&A quiz to test your knowledge about Katelyn Ohashi and her incredible journey in gymnastics!

1. How old was Katelyn Ohashi when she started gymnastics?

   a) 5 years old

   b) 3 years old

   c) 7 years old

   d) 10 years old

2. What famous routine did Katelyn perform that went viral in 2019?

   a) A routine to Disney music

   b) A routine inspired by superheroes

   c) A routine to a Michael Jackson medley

d) A routine featuring popular TikTok dances

3. What score did Katelyn receive for her viral floor routine at UCLA?

a) 9.95

b) 9.50

c) 10.0

d) 9.85

4. Why did Katelyn step away from elite gymnastics before joining UCLA?

a) She wanted to try a different sport

b) She suffered from injuries and pressure

c) She moved to another country

d) She decided to focus on school full-time

5. Which college did Katelyn attend and compete for?

a) Stanford University

b) University of Florida

c) UCLA (University of California, Los Angeles)

d) University of Michigan

6. What is Katelyn known for promoting after her gymnastics career?

a) Healthy eating

b) Traveling the world

c) Body positivity and mental health

d) Professional dancing

7. What was Katelyn's favorite part of her gymnastics routines at UCLA?

a) The flips and twists

b) The choreography and dancing

c) The dramatic final pose

d) Competing against other teams

8. How did Katelyn's gymnastics routines make her audience feel?

a) Tired

b) Bored

c) Happy and excited

d) Confused

9. What did Katelyn do after graduating from UCLA?

a) Became a professional gymnast

b) Started a new career in fashion

c) Became a motivational speaker and advocate

d) Opened her own gymnastics studio

10. What unique combination did Katelyn bring to her gymnastics performances?

a) Speed and strength

b) Comedy and stunts

c) Power and grace with lots of personality

d) Musical instruments and gymnastics

Conclusion

Katelyn Ohashi's journey from a young girl with big dreams to a global inspiration is a powerful story of resilience, self-discovery, and the pursuit of joy. Born in Seattle, Washington, Katelyn discovered her love for gymnastics at the tender age of 3. From the moment she started flipping and tumbling, it was clear that she had a special talent. Her passion for the sport drove her to excel quickly, and by her teenage years, she was competing at the highest levels of elite gymnastics.

However, the path to success was not without its challenges. As Katelyn advanced in the elite gymnastics world, she faced tremendous pressure to perform flawlessly. The intense training, the constant scrutiny, and the drive for perfection began to take a toll on her both physically and emotionally. Despite her incredible accomplishments, including winning the prestigious American Cup at just 15 years old, Katelyn struggled with injuries that threatened to end her career. She fractured her back and tore her shoulders, which forced her to step back from the sport she loved.

But what seemed like the end of her gymnastics journey was the beginning of something even more meaningful. Katelyn made the courageous decision to leave elite gymnastics behind and attend UCLA, where she joined their gymnastics team under the guidance of the legendary coach Valorie Kondos Field, known affectionately as "Miss Val." At UCLA, Katelyn found a new environment where the focus was not solely on winning but on enjoying the sport, expressing oneself, and supporting teammates.

It was at UCLA that Katelyn rediscovered her love for gymnastics. Free from the pressures of elite competition, she began to perform with a new sense of joy and creativity. Her routines were not just technically impressive; they were celebrations of life, full of energy, personality, and fun. Katelyn's approach to gymnastics became a powerful message in itself—showing that success is not just about achieving perfection but about finding happiness in what you do.

In January 2019, Katelyn's floor routine at a UCLA meeting went viral, capturing the hearts of millions around the world. Set to a medley of Michael Jackson songs, her routine was a dazzling display of athleticism, artistry, and pure joy. Katelyn didn't just perform—she danced, she smiled, and she connected with everyone who watched. The routine earned her a perfect 10.0 from the judges, but more importantly, it reminded everyone of the joy that gymnastics can bring. It wasn't just a performance; it was a statement that gymnastics—and life—should be about having fun and expressing who you truly are.

Beyond the viral fame, Katelyn's story resonated deeply with people because of her openness about the challenges she had faced. She spoke candidly about her struggles with body image, the pressures of elite gymnastics, and the importance of mental health. Katelyn used her platform to advocate for body positivity and mental wellness, encouraging others to embrace their uniqueness and prioritize their well-being. Her journey from a young gymnast chasing perfection to a strong, confident woman finding joy in her sport became an inspiration to countless individuals around the world.

After graduating from UCLA, Katelyn continued to use her voice to make a difference. She became a motivational speaker, sharing her story with audiences far and wide, inspiring them to overcome their challenges and to find happiness in their pursuits. She also became involved in various charitable causes, supporting initiatives that promote mental health, body positivity, and youth empowerment.

Katelyn's legacy extends far beyond the gymnastics mat. She has shown that true success is not about the medals you win or the records you break, but about the impact you have on others and the joy you bring to the world. Her story is a testament to the power of resilience, the importance of staying true to yourself, and the value of finding happiness in what you love.

Katelyn Ohashi's journey reminds us that life is not just about reaching the top; it's about enjoying the journey, embracing who you are, and spreading joy wherever you go. Her infectious energy, her unwavering positivity, and her commitment to helping others have made her a role model for young athletes and people everywhere. As she continues to inspire and uplift those around her, Katelyn's story will remain a shining example of what

Made in the USA
Las Vegas, NV
21 November 2024

12268305R10089